Letters
TO MY
Sacred
Romantic Partner

ELIZABETH GRIEST

Inks and Bindings
888-290-5218
www.inksandbindings.com
orders@inksandbindings.com

Contents

I 1

II 2

III...3

IV 4

V 5

VI 6

VII...7

VIII...8

IX 9

X 10

XI...11

XII...12

XIII...13

XIV 14

XV...15

XVI 16

XVII...17

XVIII...18

XIX...19

XX...20

XXII 22

XXIII 23

XXIV 24

XXV 25

XXVI 26

XXVII 27

XXVIII 28

XXIX 29

XXX 30

XXXI 31

XXXII 32

XXXIII 33

XXXIV 34

XXXV 35

XXXVI 36

XXXVII 37

XXXVIII 38

XXXIX 39

XL 40

XLI 41

XLII 42

XLIII 43

XLIV 44

XLV 45

XLVI 46

XLVII 47

XLVIII 48
XLIX 49
L..50
LI 51
LII 52
LIII 53
LIV 54

Dear Reader,

May <u>Letters To My Sacred Romantic Partner</u> bless you as much as it blesses me.

-Elizabeth Griest

I

We, Sacred partner, Believe in the Spiritual Aristocracy of the Soul Rooted in Sacred Parents of All. Mother/Father God of All.

We, Sacred partner, Believe Spiritual Aristocracy/ Nobility is not based upon wealth, formal education, or lineage; rather upon allowing Our Divine Parents of All to Guide/Guard us in living courteously/ kindly/honestly/fairly.

Further, Sacred partner, we Believe all individuals are essentially Spiritual Aristocrats/Noble for all are Children of Our Sacred Parents of All.

_____

_____

_____

_____

_____

_____

_____

_____

_____

_____

_____

II

Dear Sacred Romantic partner, you are my Sir Knight. You view me as your Fair Lady.

Sacred Partner, you are my Sir Knight, because you are a Spiritual Aristocrat/Spiritual Nobleman.

I endeavor to be a Spiritual Aristocrat/Spiritual Noblewoman.

_____

_____

_____

_____

_____

_____

_____

_____

_____

_____

_____

_____

_____

_____

_____

_____

_____

III

Sacred partner, we endeavor to live as Spiritual Aristocrats because we try to be Fair/Honest/Courteous/Kind to all.

We do our Best to Aid those we are Divinely Led to.

_____

_____

_____

_____

_____

_____

_____

_____

_____

_____

_____

_____

_____

_____

_____

_____

_____

_____

IV

Some individuals scoff at us for our Loyalty to the Spiritual Nobility Code but you, Sacred partner, and I know what's Best for us to live/do.

_____

_____

_____

_____

_____

_____

_____

_____

_____

_____

_____

_____

_____

_____

_____

_____

_____

_____

_____

_____

_____

_____

V

Sacred partner, please tell me your experience about the following:

I find the more Loyalty I demonstrate to our Spiritual Aristocracy Code the more Intuitive I grow.

Also, increased Loyalty often draws Better Circumstances, plus, more Kind/Resonant souls.

_____

_____

_____

_____

_____

_____

_____

_____

_____

_____

_____

_____

_____

_____

_____

_____

VI

Sometimes, Sacred partner, glitches occur as I endeavor to tread the Path of Spiritual Nobility.

Yet, the bumps in the road are always meant to show where some soul healing is needed.

Soul healing almost invariably involves my scared wounded Inner Child.

Does this apply to you, Sacred partner?

_____

_____

_____

_____

_____

_____

_____

_____

_____

_____

_____

_____

_____

_____

VII

Sacred partner, you and I know for our Devotion to one another to be Deep/Strong your Inner Child and my Inner Child must play a crucial role.

We also know everyone's Child Self contains one's Deepest feelings/Beliefs about oneself/others/Life/God. Also, the Inner Child holds the Blue Print of one's Divine Destiny.

The Child Self must be Devoted to the Concept of his or her Divine Destiny to be linked with his or her Sacred partner.

_____

_____

_____

_____

_____

_____

_____

_____

_____

_____

_____

VIII

Sacred partner, partially why I know you are my Divine partner is because you do not pressure me to choose or do things.

Rather, you listen attentively, ask any needful questions, then sometimes suggest something.

True, at times you strongly suggest. However, you do not force, nor threaten, nor resort to vengeance.

Sacred partner, you have my Best Interests at heart – your strong yet tender heart that beats in sync with my heart.

And, at times Heart of my heart, you utter not a word, only empathetically/kindly/lovingly smile as I speak my concerns.

Always/All Ways I am safe/secure in our Bond of Love.

A Bond no one can break.

_____

_____

_____

_____

_____

IX

Sacred partner, I can always turn to you for Comfort and Reassurance.

You can do the same with me.

Occcassionally, we may be somewhat disappointed in each other's responses.

But, we will try to understand that not even the most loving, devoted partner can always be as encouraging, comforting as one wishes.

Yet, we can always pray for one another and for us as a couple.

_____

_____

_____

_____

_____

_____

_____

_____

_____

_____

_____

X

Sacred partner, with you I am safe to live my Divine Destiny/my Sacred Life Purpose – that which I uniquely aim to live/do.

With me, Sacred partner, you are safe to live your Divine Destiny/your Sacred Life Purpose – that which you Uniquely are to live/do.

Together, Sacred partner, we are safe to live/do our Joint Divine Destiny/our Joint Sacred Life Purpose – that which we uniquely are to live/do.

XI

Sacred partner, we will always/All Ways be Truthful with one another.

Just as importantly, we will always/All Ways endeavor to be caringly/gently Truthful with each other.

_____

_____

_____

_____

_____

_____

_____

_____

_____

_____

_____

_____

_____

_____

_____

_____

_____

XII

Sacred partner, we can never be lonely as long as we communicate Heart to Heart/Soul to Soul.

At times, we may need to do so solely through Prayer and Meditation.

But, Communicate we will.

_____

_____

_____

_____

_____

_____

_____

_____

_____

_____

_____

_____

_____

_____

_____

_____

_____

_____

_____

_____

XIII

---✦·❀❀·✦---

Sacred partner, we are Bound by a Sacred Empathetic Understanding that stretches all the way back through a multitude of shared lifetimes.

Sometimes we grievously suffered, yet always we've been Bound by a Sympathetic Tie no one could destroy.

XIV

No matter who or what; you, Sacred partner, and I can always work things out, settle matters.

Yes, with Our Divine Parents of All Immutable Loving Guidance/Guardianship.

_____

_____

_____

_____

_____

_____

_____

_____

_____

_____

_____

_____

_____

_____

_____

_____

_____

_____

XV

Sacred partner, Under Divine Mercy we cast every burden upon Our Divine Parents of All.

Thus, you Sacred partner, and I go Free to continue our Divine Destiny.

_____
_____
_____
_____
_____
_____
_____
_____
_____
_____
_____
_____
_____
_____
_____
_____
_____
_____

XVI

Sacred partner, we will endeavor to always/All Ways live under Sacred Timing.

XVII

Sacred partner we will endeavor to always/all ways show gratitude for our Sacred Blessings.

Yet! Always/All Ways be open for ever increasing Divine Blessings.

_____

_____

_____

_____

_____

_____

_____

_____

_____

_____

_____

_____

_____

_____

_____

_____

_____

XVIII

Sacred partner, we will be free to laugh together, even to flirt with one another.

For, we will never be vulgar, or insulting.

Rather, we will cherish each other even in our humor.

_____

_____

_____

_____

_____

_____

_____

_____

_____

_____

_____

_____

_____

_____

_____

_____

_____

_____

_____

XIX

How I long to see you/be with you, Sacred partner.

This seeming separation wounds me so.

Yet, it must be endured/learned from/grown through until by Divine Timing we are Fully United.

_____

_____

_____

_____

_____

_____

_____

_____

_____

_____

_____

_____

_____

_____

_____

_____

_____

XX

We can be our Authentic selves with each other, Sacred partner.

Yet! through Sacred Merciful/Beautiful Courtesy.

_____

_____

_____

_____

_____

_____

_____

_____

_____

_____

_____

_____

_____

_____

_____

_____

_____

_____

_____

XXI

Shared Resonant/Right Frequency via Our Divine Parents of All is our Foundation, Sacred partner.

Our Foundation is cemented by/built upon Heart to Heart/Soul to Soul Empathetic/Courteous Communication.

_____

_____

_____

_____

_____

_____

_____

_____

_____

_____

_____

_____

_____

_____

_____

_____

_____

XXII

Sacred partner, although at times it may seem obviously redundant to do so, we daily wisely endeavor to invoke the Presence of Our Sacred Parents of All.

We are aware we need Our Divine Parents of All's Guidance/Guardianship each moment of our existence.

_____

_____

_____

_____

_____

_____

_____

_____

_____

_____

_____

_____

_____

_____

_____

XXIII

Sacred partner, we are well aware evil forces wish to drive us asunder.

However, we know we stand United under Our Sacred Parents of All's Canopy of Loving Protection/Provision.

XXIV

Sacred partner, just as we stand United under Our Divine Parents of All's Canopy of Loving Protection/Provision so do we stand United upon Their Firm Foundation of Loving Protection/ Provision.

For this, we give Them thanks.

_____

_____

_____

_____

_____

_____

_____

_____

_____

_____

_____

_____

_____

_____

_____

_____

_____

XXV

Sacred partner, we will always try to speak in gentle tones and words to each other.

If we're unable to be gentle, we'll atleast be courteous.

_____
_____
_____
_____
_____
_____
_____
_____
_____
_____
_____
_____
_____
_____
_____
_____
_____
_____
_____

XXVI

Sacred partner, I Need/Want you for the Unique Care Giving/Romance you provide me.

Sacred partner, you Need/Want me for the Unique Care Giving/Romance I provide you.

_____

_____

_____

_____

_____

_____

_____

_____

_____

_____

_____

_____

_____

_____

_____

_____

_____

_____

_____

_____

_____

_____

XXVII

I would never be afraid to request your help, Sacred partner.

For, you would never shame/blame/guilt me, nor brush me off.

Instead, you would listen attentively plus offer any practical and/or prayerful assistance you could.

_____

_____

_____

_____

_____

_____

_____

_____

_____

_____

_____

_____

_____

_____

XXVIII

Sacred partner, your Genuine Attentive Listening is Golden to me.

Because your Heartfelt Attentiveness is part of your Rock Solid Devotion to me.

_____

_____

_____

_____

_____

_____

_____

_____

_____

_____

_____

_____

_____

_____

_____

_____

_____

_____

_____

_____

XXIX

Sacred partner, you know I return your Rock Solid Devotion.

I rejoice how happy that makes you.

_____

_____

_____

_____

_____

_____

_____

_____

_____

_____

_____

_____

_____

_____

_____

_____

_____

_____

_____

XXX

At times, Sacred partner, my loneliness and sadness overwhelm me.

Then I cannot understand why you and I must be apart.

Hold me in Spirit, Sacred partner. Comfort me, Encourage me. Reassure me One day we will be United in Body as well as Soul.

Thank you, Sacred partner.

_____

_____

_____

_____

_____

_____

_____

_____

_____

_____

_____

_____

_____

_____

XXXI

Even in our most Trying Circumstances we endeavor to thank each other for our mutual devotion.

So it always be, Sacred partner.

_____

_____

_____

_____

_____

_____

_____

_____

_____

_____

_____

_____

_____

_____

_____

_____

_____

_____

_____

XXXII

It is so difficult to fathom why you, Sacred partner, have not appeared physically.

So very difficult, when you are so much a presence spiritually/emotionally/mentally.

_____

_____

_____

_____

_____

_____

_____

_____

_____

_____

_____

_____

_____

_____

_____

_____

_____

_____

_____

XXXIII

Sacred partner, one of the best aspects of our Union is the Freedom/Trust we have to tell each other the pains/disappointments we encounter in the world.

We know we can count on one another for Deep Listening/Comfort/Encouragement/Reassurance/ Practical and Prayerful Support.

_____

_____

_____

_____

_____

_____

_____

_____

_____

_____

_____

_____

_____

_____

_____

_____

XXXIV

Sometimes, Sacred partner, I feel there's no point in living without your physical presence.

But, then I think sometime/somehow/somewhere we will be Fully United.

I remember, too, I possess my Individual Sacred Destiny as well as my Joint Divine Destiny with you.

Most importantly I pray Our Sacred Parents of All Grant us, Sacred partner, our Complete Union.

_____

_____

_____

_____

_____

_____

_____

_____

_____

_____

_____

_____

_____

_____

XXXV

Sacred partner, it soothes/encourages me to affirmatively pray: My Sacred partner and I are Forever United under Divine Grace.

Pray so with me/for me, Heart of my Heart, Soul of my Soul.

_____
_____
_____
_____
_____
_____
_____
_____
_____
_____
_____
_____
_____
_____
_____
_____

XXXVI

It is Healing for me to Affirmatively pray. Forever you, Sacred partner, and I are United through Our Sacred Parents of All.

Please, you pray it, too.

_____

_____

_____

_____

_____

_____

_____

_____

_____

_____

_____

_____

_____

_____

_____

_____

_____

_____

_____

XXXVII

Sacred partner, one of your Greatest Gifts to me is your almost always empathetic understanding of my feelings/thoughts/Beliefs.

With you, I'm Freer to simply Express rather than Explain. I've had to Explain myself to so many people. Especially to individuals who are far more conventional in their thinking and Beliefs.

Of course, they're perfectly Free to be themselves.

At the same time, you and I are not only unconventional; but, also on a far more Shared Frequency: Soul Energy Based.

_____

_____

_____

_____

_____

_____

_____

_____

_____

_____

_____

XXXVIII

Sacred partner, a Great Portion of our Shared Frequency is our Valuing, Giving, and Receiving Kindness.

Of course, we can do so only imperfectly because we are not God – Our Sacred Parents of All.

In my experience and observation many individuals do not put a large emphasis on Kindness.

_____

_____

_____

_____

_____

_____

_____

_____

_____

_____

_____

_____

_____

_____

XXXIX

Sacred partner, as we so well know, Kindness is not always expressed as affection; yet, it certainly shows in True Courtesy, or at least a Genuine Attempt to demonstrate Real Courtesy.

XL

Part of why I love/need you, Sacred partner, is your assistance in treating myself with Kindness.

Plus, your help, Dear partner, in my opening up more to Divine and human Kindness.

Thank you, Sacred partner.

_____

_____

_____

_____

_____

_____

_____

_____

_____

_____

_____

_____

_____

_____

_____

_____

_____

XLI

---·◦·❈·◦·---

Sacred partner, I Want/Need a gentle man who
truly sees me/cherishes me/inspires me.

You are that man.

May Our Sacred Parents of All Unite us Quickly.

_____

_____

_____

_____

_____

_____

_____

_____

_____

_____

_____

_____

_____

_____

_____

_____

_____

_____

XLII

Sacred partner, you Want/Need a gentle woman who Truly sees you/cherishes you/inspires you.

I am that woman.

May Our Divine Parents of All Unite us Quickly.

_____

_____

_____

_____

_____

_____

_____

_____

_____

_____

_____

_____

_____

_____

_____

_____

_____

_____

_____

XLIII

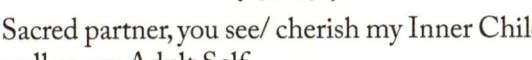

Sacred partner, you see/ cherish my Inner Child as well as my Adult Self.

You Inspire my Inner Child and Adult Self.

Pray with me we're soon Joined via Our Sacred Parents of All.

XLIV

Sacred partner, i see/cherish your Inner Child, as well as your Adult Self.

I inspire your Inner Child plus your Adult Self.

I pray with you we're soon Joined through Our Divine Parents of All.

_____

_____

_____

_____

_____

_____

_____

_____

_____

_____

_____

_____

_____

_____

_____

_____

_____

_____

_____

XLV

Sacred partner, we agree we will not engage in physical intimacy unless/until we marry.

My Inner Child/I need to feel Safe/Secure in order to have total intimacy of body/mind/soul.

To experience Safety/Security I need Total Commitment/Devotion from my husband.

_____

_____

_____

_____

_____

_____

_____

_____

_____

_____

_____

_____

_____

_____

_____

_____

XLVI

Sacred partner, sometimes the best choice we can make for ourselves is simply agree to disagree.

And, to do so with as much loving courtesy as we can muster.

_____

_____

_____

_____

_____

_____

_____

_____

_____

_____

_____

_____

_____

_____

_____

_____

_____

_____

_____

XLVII

---❖❖❖---

However, Sacred partner, agreeing to disagree doesn't mean we ignore decisions that must be made, nor issues that have to be more thoroughly discussed.

Thus, it would be best to pray over them. Then endeavor to find/act upon Sacred solutions which benefit you and me.

_____

_____

_____

_____

_____

_____

_____

_____

_____

_____

_____

_____

_____

_____

XLVIII

Sacred partner, we help each other in s myriad of ways.

One is suggesting to each other courteous methods of dealing with troublesome individuals.

Of course, as in all our interactions to go through Our Divine Parents of All.

_____

_____

_____

_____

_____

_____

_____

_____

_____

_____

_____

_____

_____

_____

_____

_____

_____

_____

_____

_____

XLIX

Sacred partner, it is so Reassuring to know/ experience we are free always to offer gentle suggestions to one another.

Yes, always via Our Sacred Parents of All.

_____

_____

_____

_____

_____

_____

_____

_____

_____

_____

_____

_____

_____

_____

_____

_____

_____

_____

L

Sacred partner, although we have not met in the flesh; perhaps we never will, still, we influence/uplift each other via our Soul Frequencies through Our Sacred Parents of All: Mother/Father God of All.

_____

_____

_____

_____

_____

_____

_____

_____

_____

_____

_____

_____

_____

_____

_____

_____

_____

_____

_____

_____

_____

LI

Everyday, Sacred partner, I remind myself you love me, Sacred Parents of All love me.

Knowing/Thinking/Feeling that is my Lifeline.

_____

_____

_____

_____

_____

_____

_____

_____

_____

_____

_____

_____

_____

_____

_____

_____

_____

_____

_____

_____

LII

Please, Sacred Partner, Everyday remind yourself I love you, Sacred Parents of All love you.

Please let that be your Lifeline.

_____
_____
_____
_____
_____
_____
_____
_____
_____
_____
_____
_____
_____
_____
_____
_____
_____
_____
_____
_____

LIII

How fortunate we are, Sacred partner, to Know/Feel/Believe Sacred Partnership Exists.

How equally fortunate we are, Sacred partner, to Know/Feel/Believe Our Sacred Parents of All Exist.

_____

_____

_____

_____

_____

_____

_____

_____

_____

_____

_____

_____

_____

_____

_____

_____

_____

LIV

How fortunate we are, Sacred Partner, to Know/ Feel/Believe one day you and I will be Fully United via Our Sacred Parents of All/Our Mother/ Father God of All.

_____

_____

_____

_____

_____

_____

_____

_____

_____

_____

_____

_____

_____

_____

_____

_____

_____

_____

_____

_____

www.ingramcontent.com/pod-product-compliance
Lightning Source LLC
Chambersburg PA
CBHW020341130626
46549CB00003B/1239